CRYSTAL LAKE SCHOOL LIBRARY

D1432758

598.97   c.1
SAT   Sattler, Helen Roney
        The Book of North American
Owls

CRYSTAL LAKE SCHOOL LIBRARY

DEMCO

THE BOOK OF
NORTH AMERICAN

OWLS

spotted owl

CRYSTAL LAKE SCHOOL LIBRARY

THE BOOK OF
NORTH AMERICAN

OWLS

by Helen Roney Sattler
illustrated by Jean Day Zallinger

CLARION BOOKS/NEW YORK

Dedicated to Frances and George
with greatest affection

I wish to express my deepest appreciation and sincere thanks to Dr. Steve K. Sherrod, director of the George Sutton Avian Research Center, Inc., near Bartlesville, Oklahoma, for reading the complete manuscript and providing many valuable pieces of information, and for checking the drawings for accuracy.

Clarion Books
a Houghton Mifflin Company imprint
215 Park Avenue South, New York, NY 10003
Text copyright © 1995 by Helen Roney Sattler
Illustrations copyright © 1995 by Jean Day Zallinger

The illustrations for this book were
executed in watercolors and color
pencils on Strathmore Coldpress.
The text was set in 12pt.-Trump Medieval

All rights reserved.

For information about permission to reproduce selections from this book, write to Permission Houghton Mifflin Company, 215 Park Avenue South, New York, NY 10003.

Printed in Singapore

Library of Congress Cataloging-in-Publication Data
Sattler, Helen Roney.
    The book of North American owls / by Helen Roney Sattler; illustrated by Jean Day Zallinger.
        p.   cm.
    Includes bibliographical references and index.
    Summary: Provides general information on the behavior of owls and specific information about the physical characteristics and behavior of the twenty-one North American species.
    ISBN 0-395-60524-5
    1. Owls—North America—Juvenile literature. [1. Owls.] I. Zallinger, Jean, ill. II. Title.
QL696.S8S28 1994
598'.97'097—dc20   91-43636
                                                                      CIP
                                                                       AC

TWP   10 9 8 7 6 5 4 3 2 1

Contents

CHAPTER 1

What Is an Owl?

The spring before I started school, my younger brother and I discovered that the barn was a perfect place to play on windy days when it was too cold to play outside. We were protected from the wind, and the hay kept the temperature warmer inside than out. The barn was also a perfect roosting place for the big barn owl that perched on its nest box high above our heads.

Even though the owl seemed half as tall as we were, we weren't afraid of it. I was fascinated by its heart-shaped face and by the way it watched our every move with its big eyes, turning its head from side to side.

But Dad didn't like the owl in his barn. He said it brought mites and that its droppings and pellets made a mess and spoiled the hay. He tried, with little success, to discourage us from playing out there. He said it wasn't safe.

Dad may have been afraid the owl would attack us during nesting season. Owls can be quite belligerent when protecting their nests. Eventually Dad tore the nest box down, and the owl found another suitable nesting place nearby. I still heard its familiar calls just after dusk.

Many people don't like owls because they are raptors—birds of prey that catch other animals for food. At one time, farmers shot every owl they saw because owls sometimes killed chickens and geese. Most people, however, are as fascinated by and respectful of owls as I am. Pictures and stories show us that people have

carved wood owl head
North Coast Indians

been captivated by these unusual birds throughout history. Ancient people who believed that owls were spirits and had magic powers either worshiped or feared the birds. Pictures of owls were drawn on the walls of caves eighteen thousand years ago by ancient Europeans and by prehistoric Native Americans in Tennessee. Today, the owl is considered a symbol of wisdom, maybe because of its large, staring eyes, or perhaps because it usually sits quietly, observing everything that goes on without making a sound.

There are a lot of things to admire about owls. If it were not for owls, there would be much less food for humans to eat. Owls destroy enormous numbers of pests, such as rodents and insects, that eat crops and damage grain. They are the world's greatest mousers and are the cheapest and most efficient natural controllers of rodent populations available: They cost nothing. Owls deserve the strict protection they now get.

Until recently, no one knew very much about owls. Owls are seldom seen and had not been well studied because of the difficulty of observing them. Most owls are nocturnal birds (they hunt at night and roost during the day), and many live in remote forested habitats. When people finally began to understand the value of owls, laws were passed to protect these birds and funds provided to pay scientists to study them. Most of what we now know about owls has been learned in the last fifteen years.

Owls come in all sizes and shapes. They live throughout the world on every continent except Antarctica and are found in every kind of habitat, from cold Arctic tundra to hot tropical forests and from arid prairies to wet marshlands.

Scientists call all soft-plumaged, short-tailed, big-headed birds of prey with flat facial disks and large, forward-facing eyes owls. The word *owl* comes from the Old English word *ule*, meaning "to howl," and refers to the birds' distinctive calls. Scientists divide all living things into different groups, or orders. The order of owls is Strigiformes (STRIG-ih-forms), from *striges*, the name of a Greek owl.

There are two families, or kinds, of Strigiformes. Most owls belong to the Strigidae (STRIG-ih-dee) family, the typical owls. They range in length (from the top of the head to the tip of the

carved stone owl
Mexico, early Mayan

TYTONIDAE

barn owl
14–20 in

STRIGIDAE

great
gray owl
24–33 in

great
horned
owl
18–25 in

snowy owl
21–30 in

spotted owl
16–19 in

tail) from five to thirty-three inches. The smallest weighs about as much as a mockingbird (1 to 1.4 ounce); the largest weighs as much as a black vulture (3.5 to 4.4 pounds). There are 130 species of Strigidae. Twenty-one of them live in North America.

The other family is called the Tytonidae (ty-TON-ih-dee), or barn owls. The name Tytonidae comes from the Greek word *tuto*, meaning "night owl," which fits barn owls very well because they hunt only at night. They are rarely seen in the daytime except when roosting in a barn. Barn owls are different from other owls in several ways. Their facial disks are heart-shaped; their eyes are smaller than those of typical owls; and their ear openings are ovals instead of slits. Their legs are longer than those of the Strigidae, and a barn owl's second toe is the same length as its first toe. Their high-pitched call is different too. Barn owls don't hoot like most typical owls. There are twelve kinds of Tytonidae, but only one lives in North America.

ferruginous
pygmy-owl
6.5–7 in

flammulated
owl
6–7 in

vermiculated
screech owl
8–9 in

eastern
screech owl
7–10 in

short-
eared
owl
13–17 in

barred owl
16–24 in

long-eared owl
13–16 in

northern
hawk owl
14–17 in

whiskered
screech owl
6.5–8 in

western
screech owl
6–9.2 in

northern
pygmy-owl
7–7.5 in

northern
saw-whet
owl
7–8.5 in

boreal owl
8–12 in

burrowing
owl
8.5–11 in

elf owl
5–6 in

mountain
pygmy-owl
5.5–6.5 in

THE TWO FAMILIES OF NORTH AMERICAN OWLS
ORGANIZED BY SIZE (Body Length Given)

9

Scientists separate families into genera and species, which are given scientific names that are the same throughout the world in every language. The North American barn owl's scientific name is *Tyto alba* (*Tyto*, the genus name, is Greek for "night owl," and *alba*, the species name, is Latin for "white"). The name tells us it is a white night owl.

Not everyone agrees on the exact number of species of owls in the world today. The most recent checklist names one hundred sixty-four. Of these, only twenty-one live in North America.

Owls have been around for a very long time, much longer than humans. They probably became distinct from other birds seventy to eighty million years ago, while dinosaurs were still roaming the earth. The fossil record of owls is one of the longest of all groups of living birds. The owl generally accepted as oldest is *Ogygoptynx* (oh-JIG-op-tinks). It was named for Ogyges (oh-JIG-ez), the Greek mythical king of Thebes, and the Greek name of an owl, *ptynx*. It lived in Colorado more than sixty million years ago. We can't be sure what it looked like because it is known only from an ankle and foot, but these parts are very similar to those of the modern burrowing owl. The burrowing owl eats insects and reptiles. Scientists think *Ogygoptynx* probably also ate insects and reptiles. Fossil evidence suggests its ancestors may have come from Asia.

barn owl

unfeathered head

ear flap

asymmetrical skull

ear opening

ear opening

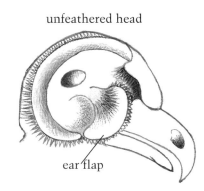

feathers near ear flap

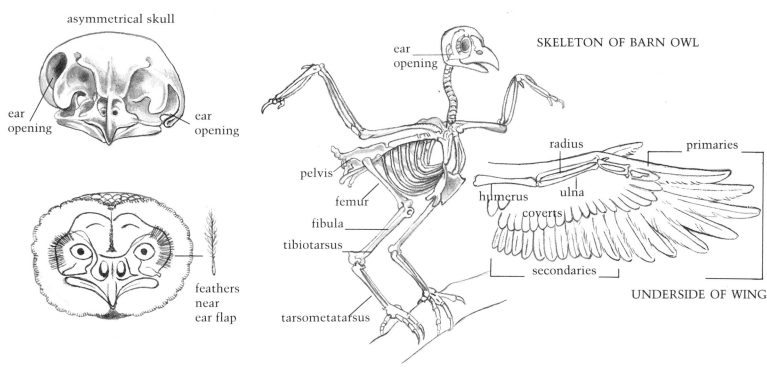

ear opening

SKELETON OF BARN OWL

pelvis

femur

fibula

tibiotarsus

tarsometatarsus

radius

humerus

ulna

coverts

primaries

secondaries

UNDERSIDE OF WING

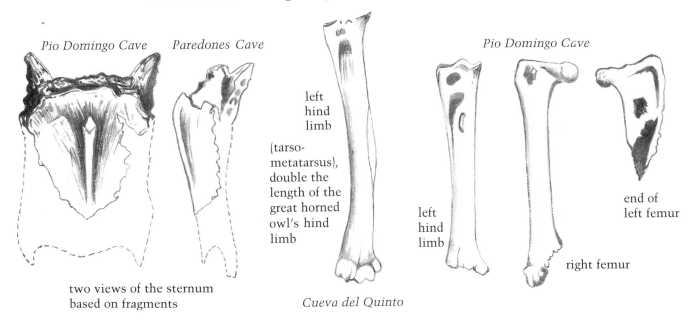

Pio Domingo Cave *Paredones Cave*

left hind limb (tarso-metatarsus), double the length of the great horned owl's hind limb

Pio Domingo Cave

left hind limb

end of left femur

right femur

two views of the sternum based on fragments

Cueva del Quinto

Protostrix (PRO-toh-striks) is the next oldest fossil owl. Its name means "first owl" in Greek. Although it was not the first owl, it was the oldest known when it was named. It lived in Wyoming between thirty-eight and fifty-four million years ago. The feet of *Protostrix* were designed for seizing and killing mammals. Fossils of a small terrier-sized horse, *Eohippus*, were found nearby. *Protostrix*, a possible ancestor of barn owls, may have preyed upon *Eohippus*.

It is not known for sure where or exactly when barn owls originated. The earliest known barn owl, *Sophiornis* (SO-fih-OR-nis), lived in France about twenty-four million years ago. The largest barn owl, *Tyto riveroi*, lived in Cuba thirty thousand years ago. It was between two and three times the size of barn owls living in Cuba today.

Ornimegalonyx (Or-nih-MEG-ah-lon-iks), the largest owl that ever lived, was twice the size of the great horned owl. This ten-thousand-year-old owl was capable of killing giant sloths and pig-sized rodents, as scientists know from bones found with it in a cave in Cuba.

It was once thought that owls were relatives of falcons and hawks because they resemble them in some ways. However, it is now known that the similarities came about only because both types of birds have developed tools that all flying hunters need. The owls' nearest living relatives are whippoorwills and nighthawks.

nighthawk

whippoorwill

CHAPTER 2

Perfect Predators

Shortly after sunset, a barn owl awakens and leaves its perch. Silently it patrols the pasture, skimming over the ground just a few feet above the vegetation, looking and listening for small animals. Spotting a meadow mouse, it hovers momentarily; then, with its talons spread, it plunges and lands on the animal, pinning it to the ground. The owl kills the mouse with its beak and swallows it whole.

This owl is lucky—it captured food on its first attempt of the night. Studies show that most owls miss more often than they catch prey. Although owls are superb hunters, the animals they feed on are skillful at escaping. Owls seldom go hungry, however, except in winter, because food is usually plentiful during other seasons and owls are well equipped for catching it.

Most owls' legs are covered with feathers. Below these "trousers" of feathers on each foot are four powerful toes equipped with long, curved, needle-sharp talons. Two of these toes can turn forward and the other two backward, enabling the owl to get a firm grip on its prey. Once grasped, the prey seldom gets loose. A great horned owl's grip may be one of the strongest in nature. It can snap the neck of a groundhog as easily as you can a toothpick. Most owls, however, kill by biting their prey at the base of the skull with sharp, hooked beaks.

Owls are also well equipped for finding food. With the exception of the short-eared owl, the snowy owl—which lives in

curved talons overlap
to grip prey firmly

darker area indicates scope of owl's binocular (three-dimensional) vision. Each eye can also see to the side (lighter area)

OWL EYE

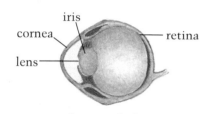

daytime (light)

nighttime (dark)

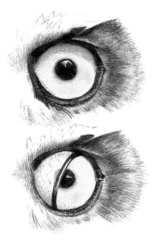

nictitating membrane

the far north where nights are sometimes very short—and the burrowing owl, owls hunt at night, going to work just as other birds are going to roost. They are magnificent night hunters. Though they can see very well in daylight, they can see much better in the dark—many times better than humans can. Large eyes collect more light than small eyes, and their eyes are huge. The eyes of a seventy-ounce snowy owl weigh as much as those of a two-hundred-pound man. They take up more space in the owl's head than its thimble-sized brain.

In addition, an owl's eyes are placed in the front of its head and spaced far apart. This gives the owl excellent binocular, or three-dimensional, vision, which allows it to judge accurately distances as well as the size and speed of its prey. A great gray owl is able to spot a mouse two hundred yards (the length of two football fields) away.

Owls can also change the focus of their eyes rapidly. They can focus on objects both near and far at the same time. This may be why they can fly through tree branches at night and not collide with them. In addition to upper and lower lids, owls have a third, translucent eyelid called a nictitating (NIK-tuh-tayt-ing) membrane. This membrane keeps the eye moist and may give protection from damage during struggles with prey. Tests show that some owls can distinguish between colors.

Owls cannot roll or turn their eyeballs in their eye sockets as humans can, because their eyes are tube-shaped instead of ball-shaped. To follow prey, an owl must turn its head or raise or lower it, but this is no problem for an owl. Though short, their necks are extraordinarily flexible. Owls have fourteen neck vertebrae, seven more than most birds. These extra vertebrae allow an owl to swivel its head like a radar scanner, 180 degrees to the right or left, so that the head sometimes appears to be on backward. An owl can also turn its face completely upside down or flip it back so that its crown touches its shoulders.

upper and lower eyelids

daytime (light)

nighttime (dark)

SHORT-EARED OWL

Owls have extra sensitive ears. Their hearing is probably among the best in the animal world. Some species depend more on hearing their prey than on seeing it. A great gray owl can hear a beetle running through grass a hundred feet away (more than the length of a basketball court) or the squeak of a mouse a half mile distant.

Most owls' external ears are large slits hidden behind their facial disks. The facial disks are made of long, soft-edged feathers fastened into the rims of the ear slits. Though the facial disks are what make owls look like owls, their main function is to act as dish antennae. They trap sounds, concentrate them, and funnel them into the ear. An owl can turn or move its facial disks to improve the reception.

The eyes of a great gray owl are smaller than those of most owls, but the facial disks are enormous, and these birds have remarkable hearing. Great gray owls can locate and capture live prey deep beneath snow, or even underground, by sound alone. Like most owls, a great gray will sit patiently on a tree branch all night, if necessary, cocking its head from side to side and listening intently. An observer once saw a great gray suddenly and silently drop from its roost and hover momentarily over a gopher's burrow. Then, reaching down with its legs, the owl crashed through the feeding tunnel, grasped the unseen animal in its talons, and returned to its branch.

The ears of some owls are placed asymmetrically—one ear is lower than the other—and are of different sizes. The right ear hears sound best from below. The left ear hears sound best from above. This adaptation helps the owl to locate prey with astonishing pinpoint accuracy. Studies show that a blindfolded owl can fly directly to prey that it cannot see, and grasp it in its talons. The slightest movement or sound will alert an owl to get into position to swoop down on its prey.

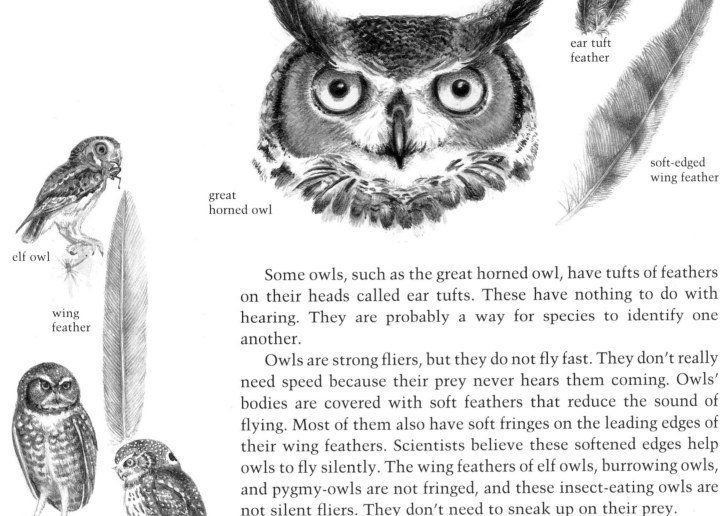

ear tuft feather

soft-edged wing feather

great horned owl

elf owl

wing feather

burrowing owl

pygmy-owl

Some owls, such as the great horned owl, have tufts of feathers on their heads called ear tufts. These have nothing to do with hearing. They are probably a way for species to identify one another.

Owls are strong fliers, but they do not fly fast. They don't really need speed because their prey never hears them coming. Owls' bodies are covered with soft feathers that reduce the sound of flying. Most of them also have soft fringes on the leading edges of their wing feathers. Scientists believe these softened edges help owls to fly silently. The wing feathers of elf owls, burrowing owls, and pygmy-owls are not fringed, and these insect-eating owls are not silent fliers. They don't need to sneak up on their prey.

Like those of all birds, owls' bones are light—the bones of a seventy-ounce snowy owl weigh no more than six ounces. Although the bones are full of air pockets, they are strong because they are crossbraced with solid shafts. The wings of most owls are broad and very strong. They are huge in relation to the body because they must be able to lift both the bird and any prey it catches.

front of pygmy-owl

back of pygmy-owl showing eyespots

head turned all the way front to back

Most owls are opportunistic hunters and will eat anything that is plentiful and easy to catch. They eat rats, mice, and other small rodents because these are nearly always plentiful. Owls also eat rabbits, squirrels, prairie dogs, skunks, lemmings, birds, reptiles, and amphibians, and some eat insects, spiders, scorpions, and worms. Owls vary greatly in size. A two-and-a-half-foot-long great gray owl is six times larger than a five-inch-long elf owl. It requires more food and usually goes after bigger prey. Great horned owls and snowy owls might catch prey as large as raccoons or snowshoe rabbits. The smallest owls usually prefer insects, earthworms, and small reptiles.

Owls usually swallow small prey whole, headfirst. Larger prey is usually torn apart before swallowing. Unlike many other birds, owls don't have crops—pouched enlargements of the gullet where digestion begins—and cannot digest hair, feathers, or bony material as well as hawks can, for example. Much of this material is regurgitated, or spit up, in pellets. The size and shape of the pellets vary with the type of owl. Scientists can often determine which owl spit up a pellet by studying its shape and contents. They can also learn what the owl has eaten.

An owl's prey rarely sees its captor because owls are well camouflaged. They vary greatly in color and markings, but all are patterned so that they blend well into their surroundings. Most of them are combinations of brown, gray, black, and white. Their eyes are either dark brown or yellow. Males and females are usually marked alike. Female snowy owls, however, have more dark barring on their breasts and backs than males; this helps camouflage them when on the nest.

CHAPTER 3

Courtship and Nesting

"**H**OOOOO! Who, who, who, HOO HOO!" A great horned owl is advertising for a mate. "Come and see, I have a good, safe territory with a fine nesting site and plenty of prey," he is saying. Soon an unattached female checks him out and looks over what he has to offer. If she likes what she sees, she will answer his call with a slightly higher-pitched one, and their courtship ritual will begin.

Owls spend a long time courting. Great horned owls hoot back and forth for several nights. Then the female flies to a tree near that of the male. They continue hooting for several more weeks while getting acquainted. Eventually they hoot in duet. Scientists think that duetting bonds the pair together. Finally they light in the same tree, and with much purring, gurgling, and ruffling of feathers, bow to and begin preening each other. After a while the male offers the female a freshly caught rabbit or rodent. Then the owls begin their courtship dance, hopping from branch to branch while slowly rotating their bodies and lifting and overlapping their wings again and again.

Not all courtship rituals are as involved as that of the great horned owl, but all owls go through a lengthy courtship before mating. Although the rituals may be similar in some respects, each species' ritual is slightly different from the others. Barn owls, for example, do most of their courting in the air. The male soars above his hunting territory while uttering long-drawn-out screeches similar to those of wailing cats. When an interested

female joins him in the air, he pursues her, attempting to lure her into a nesting site. If the female accepts the nest, they both fly to it and begin fencing with their bills and rubbing their cheeks together, much as a cat rubs against your leg. The male short-eared owl's aerial display is similar to that of the barn owl, but this owl claps its wings together while circling over its hunting territory.

Body postures, touching, preening, cheek rubbing, and wing overlapping during courtship are forms of communication. Owls communicate in a variety of other ways. Long-distance communications are vocal. Most owls hoot, but the calls of some (the screech owl and barn owl, for example) are more like screams. A male's voice is usually deeper than that of the female and carries farther. A male snowy owl's voice can be heard seven miles away.

Some owls are seldom heard, while others are noisy year round. The noisiest seasons are autumn, when males are establishing hunting territories, and late winter or early spring, when owls are courting. On a clear, moonlit night hoots may be heard all night long. Each species has its own style of hooting, with a combination of short and long hoots somewhat like the dots and dashes of Morse code. These special hooting patterns help owls identify other members of their species.

All owls have a rather large vocabulary of sounds and calls, each with a different meaning. One call is used for advertising ownership of territories. Another is used for attracting a mate. Still another is used for duetting during courtship.

Duetting, preening, and courtship feeding are common among most owls and are recognized by scientists as important parts of courtship activities. Courtship begins only after an adult male has established a hunting territory and announced his ownership by nightly hooting. To all other owls of the same species, this call clearly says, "This is my space. Keep out."

By the time they are a year old, most owls are mature, and the males begin seeking an unoccupied territory the next fall. To be suitable, the territory must have enough prey to feed two adults and their young. Its size varies with the size of the owl, the number of offspring the owl produces, and the abundance of food in the territory. A great horned owl may require up to one thousand acres, while a flammulated owl can manage with as little as seven and a half acres and a great gray owl needs just a few hundred square feet.

Most owls prefer living in wild regions near the edges of forests, far from human interference. Barn owls and screech owls, however, don't mind living near humans because there is nearly always a good supply of rats and mice where there are humans.

great
horned owls
roosting

Males hoot to learn if a territory is unoccupied. If their hoots are answered, they know that other owls are present. If no one answers, the young male will claim the area for his own. If he is answered by a feeble call, the young male may try to drive the current resident out. The takeover battle will probably be a bloodless hooting and chasing contest. Few owls engage in face-to-face combat because most healthy owls, equipped with deadly weapons, defend their territories fiercely. Most owls find a territory near where they were hatched. They rarely need to go farther than six and a half miles. However, evidence from tagged birds shows that some have traveled as far as seventy miles before establishing a territory.

A good roosting place near the hunting area is almost as important as a good food supply. The roosting spot should be well hidden and should provide some protection from the weather, because the owl will spend all day, year round, on the roost, sleeping and digesting its last meal. Most owls choose a crevice, natural cavity, or tree branch hidden by thick foliage for a roosting site. Barn owls often roost on their nests. Short-eared and snowy owls, however, sometimes roost on the ground in clumps of tall grass, because they often live in areas where there are few trees. Ground roosters seldom rest in the same place twice, but most other owls will occupy their favorite sleeping places for long periods, maybe even years.

short-eared owl
roosting

Owls are vulnerable while sleeping because they may not hear or see an approaching enemy. Hawks, crows, and jays mob-attack any owl that they find asleep in a tree. Although owls are usually stronger than these birds, they have difficulty defending themselves against a mob. An owl's best defense in such cases is to avoid being seen in the first place. If an owl remains perfectly still near the trunk of a tree, it will blend into the background and go unnoticed. Some owls flatten their feathers and stand up as tall as possible, so that their long, thin outlines look more like broken-off stumps than like owls.

great horned owl

Owls doze periodically during the day, usually drooping their heads slightly onto their breasts. Small owls may twist their heads around and rest them on their backs.

Most owls are not social birds and rarely allow another of their species into their hunting territories during nesting season. Members of some species, however, tend to come together to sleep. The group may consist of a mated pair and their offspring, or perhaps several owls roosting together for protection, as is the case with short-eared owls. On the other hand, they could be roosting in the same place simply because that is the best roosting site available.

short-eared owls

great
horned
owl

great
gray owl

elf owls

The home territory also needs to have one or more suitable nesting sites close to the hunting area. Owls rarely, if ever, build their own nests. Many of them simply take over abandoned nests of hawks, crows, herons, or squirrels. The female owl may add a few pine needles or strips of bark to line the nest but more often doesn't bother to do even that. Other owls prefer to nest in natural cavities such as hollow trees, holes in stumps, old woodpecker nests, rock ledges, or crevices in cliffs. Barn owls and screech owls like abandoned buildings, barns, church steeples, bridges, and sometimes birdhouses. Desert-living burrowing owls usually nest in old mammal burrows. If they can't find an unoccupied burrow, they may dig one of their own. Snowy owls and short-eared owls usually nest on the ground, scraping out shallow spots on high ground, which they sometimes line with grass.

Most owls don't begin nesting until they are two years old. Great grays may be four years old. Although the male usually makes the initial selection of a nesting site, it is the female that makes the final decision. Mated pairs often stay together for many years—a pair of barred owls stayed together twenty-six years. If the nest proves to be a good one, a long-established pair may use it for twenty years or more.

snowy owl

burrowing owl

CHAPTER 4

Baby Owls

As soon as a pair of owls has selected a nesting site, they mate and the female begins laying eggs. Large owls usually lay only two eggs, while small owls may lay seven or eight. In some species the clutch size varies from year to year, depending upon the food supply. A snowy owl may produce up to fourteen eggs in years when food is plentiful and none in years when prey is scarce.

The size of the egg also varies greatly from one species to another. A great horned owl's egg is about the size of a chicken's egg. The egg of a pygmy-owl is less than half as big. The eggs are pure white, and most are nearly round.

Owls living in warm climates may lay eggs anytime during the year, but northern species often don't start laying before February. Most owls deposit eggs in the nest two to four days apart. Every North American owl, except the pygmy-owl, begins incubating, or sitting on the eggs to keep them warm, as soon as the first egg is laid. The incubation period can be rather long, from twenty-one to thirty-five days. The female does most, if not all, of the incubating. The male's job during incubation is to defend the nest against predators and his territory against other owls. He also feeds the female while she incubates. The female seldom leaves the nest, because the eggs might get too cold if left unattended for even a short time. In colder regions, a male will sometimes keep the eggs warm while the female takes breaks.

A male will attack nearly any intruder, regardless of size, that gets too close to his nest. Some male owls spread their wings, snap their bills, and fluff their feathers until they look twice their actual size. Others dive at an intruder's head and flap around it.

great gray owl

Hikers, unaware that they were near an owl's nest, have received stunning blows on the head from a silent attacker's beating wings. If a fox or raccoon comes too near the nest, a parent owl may pretend to be injured. Dropping to the ground and fluttering about as if it had a broken wing, the owl lures the intruder away from the nest. As soon as it is safe to do so, the parent owl returns to the nest. Adult owls are even more aggressive toward intruders when the eggs start hatching.

owl egg   egg tooth   owlet's appearance inside egg

a few hours old

When an owl chick is ready to hatch, it pecks a small round hole in the egg with its "egg tooth"—a small spur that every baby bird has near the tip of its beak. This is hard work, and the effort wears the owlet out. After it breaks the initial hole, the owlet may not be ready to break out of the shell completely for as long as two days.

Newly hatched chicks are rather unattractive. Most are nearly naked and so weak they can barely hold up their enormous heads. Their huge bulging eyes are sealed shut. Newly hatched owlets range in size from a half-inch-long elf owlet to a baby-chick-sized great horned owlet. The owlets gain strength rapidly. Their appetites are enormous, and they begin to clamor for food almost immediately. The father bird is kept busy feeding his hungry young.

young barn owls

Since the eggs are laid several days apart and incubation begins with the first egg laid, hatching is staggered. The first owlet to hatch in a large clutch may be two weeks old before the last one breaks out of its egg. Unlike most birds of prey, owlets seldom quarrel in the nest. However, if prey is scarce, the older and stronger owlets get most of the food and are more likely to live to maturity. Staggered hatching is one of nature's ways of ensuring that surviving chicks are strong and well fed.

Staggered hatching also lessens the burden on the parent birds. The mother bird broods the newly hatched babies for up to three weeks by snuggling up to them and spreading her wings over them to keep them warm. During this time the father bird often accumulates a large stock of surplus food near the nest.

The chicks are able to swallow insects whole, but the mother owl strips hair and bones from larger prey, then tears the meat to bits for the young. Bits of the food and owlet droppings fall to the bottom of the nest. In open nests they fall to the ground through cracks, but tree-hole nests can become quite messy. Most owls are not good housekeepers and seldom bother to clean their nests. Some eastern screech owls, however, keep their nests tidy with the help of "live-in maids." They capture small blind snakes and drop them into their nests with the chicks. The blind snakes devour maggots and other insects that feed on the droppings and food scraps. Although screech owls are fond of snakes as food, they seldom eat their blind-snake maids.

small
blind
snake

eastern screech owls

screech owls

Owlets growing up in clean homes are healthier, grow faster, and survive better than owlets living in insect-infested nests. Within a few hours of hatching, the coats of healthy owlets have fluffed out to be thick velvety coats of white or sooty down. The chicks soon look like soft, cuddly balls of fluff. They are rather comical in their actions and appearance at this stage. Within two to four weeks, depending upon the size of the species, the oldest have developed enough reserves of body fat to keep themselves warm. Then the mother owl joins the father in bringing prey to their hungry young, who constantly beg for food with shrieks, grunts, clicks, buzzes, wheezes, and snaps. Now the mother only visits the nest to drop off food. The oldest owlets sometimes keep the youngest warm. Young barn owlets may even try to feed their younger nest mates.

spider

beetle

mouse   shrew   rabbit   frog   31

just hatched

ten weeks later

juvenile

eastern
screech
owl

red-brown
phase

gray phase

As the young grow, they become more alert and can move about the nest. They can swallow prey whole, and their parents start bringing them larger prey. With a large brood, feeding the young can be a lot of work. One pair of barn owls killed over fifteen hundred rodents in one season to feed their young and themselves.

As the owlets grow, they shed their first down and begin growing juvenile plumage and wing and tail feathers. While these grow in, the chicks go through an "ugly duckling" stage, but as soon as they are fully feathered, they look almost exactly like their parents.

Some owls come in two distinct color patterns. Western screech owls are usually gray, while eastern screech owls may be either red-brown or gray. Their color is determined by genetics, and red is dominant just as it is with red-headed humans.

Owlets cannot fly until they are almost completely feathered and their wing and tail feathers are fully developed. These long, narrow feathers move the birds forward and provide lift. They are shorter, more rounded, and softer in owls than in other birds of equal size. Soft body feathers preserve heat and make the owlets streamlined and silent fliers.

snowy owls

Although small species of owls can fly as soon as they leave the nest, they, like all owlets, do a good deal of "branching"—hopping from branch to branch or wandering on the ground near the nest—before they actually start flying. During branching, the owlets learn to identify sight and sound signals necessary for survival. They also exercise and strengthen their wings by flapping them, and engage in vocabulary-building sessions. They try out every sound their little voice boxes are capable of, sometimes experimenting all night long. Occasionally a branching owlet falls to the ground. Most are unable to fly back to the nest. Some return to the tree by using their talons and beaks to climb the tree trunk; others remain on the ground and are fed there by their parents.

Many owlets spend a long time on the forest floor before they can fly well. Great horned fledglings spend ten days to two weeks hopping about in the branches or on the ground. Their parents bring them food and guide them in experimental hunting. They also guard them against predators, ready to plunge their deadly talons into anything that bothers their babies.

Barn owlets are seldom bothered by predators and develop more slowly than other species. They reach full adult weight when they are six weeks old, but are not fully feathered until they are sixty-six days old. They leave the nest and begin exploring their surroundings when they are four weeks old, and fly at eight to ten weeks. Long-eared owlets reach their full adult weight at three to four weeks, leave the nest at twenty-three to twenty-six days, and fly at five weeks old.

The first flight takes longer for big owls than for small ones, and owlets who have hatched on the ground leave their nests sooner and are able to fly sooner than those hatched in trees. Elf owlets can fly within twenty-seven days of hatching. It may take great horned owlets seventy days to become airborne.

Once they can fly, owlets may catch some of their food for themselves, but their parents continue to feed them. The owlets will not be able to make it on their own until well into autumn. It takes months of trial and error to become skillful hunters. Even the largest species start by catching insects and small reptiles. Species that eat mostly insects are on their own much sooner than those that eat larger vertebrate prey.

Some owl families tend to stay together throughout the first winter. Others scatter, and their owlets begin to seek vacant territories as soon as they are independent.

barn owls

long-eared owls

CHAPTER 5

The Future for Owls

Not all owlets reach adulthood. Fifty percent die in their first year. A few young are taken by predators, but the most common cause of death is starvation. If food is scarce, young owls are the first to suffer. Adult owls can move to areas where food is plentiful. They can compete for and defend hunting territories. Young owls can't, and have a harder time. If they are lucky enough to survive to adulthood, they have a chance at a good long life.

Most owls prefer to stay in one range year round. A few owls move from higher altitudes to lower altitudes, and some may move from the northern edge of their range to a little farther south in winter, but none travel great distances except to follow the food supply.

A large owl living in a wilderness area with a good food supply might survive up to thirty years. Well-fed and protected zoo owls sometimes live to be fifty to sixty years old. Large owls live longer than small ones. The longest-lived owl known—an African eagle owl—was sixty-eight years old when it died.

Adult owls have few enemies besides humans. Some large owls prey on smaller ones, but the owl's greatest natural enemy is the goshawk. Scientific studies of great horned owls show that 96 percent of dead adult birds were killed by humans. Most were shot or trapped, some were hit by automobiles—forty-five in a single twenty-four-hour period in Idaho—and a few were electrocuted on power lines. Spraying of cotton crops in Arizona kills large numbers of elf owls each year. In the midwest, many die from

African eagle owl

goshawk

eating rodents that have fed on wheat treated with dieldrin, an insecticide related to DDT—a powerful insecticide once used to dust crops. Rodent-control programs also cause problems for burrowing owls in the southwest, and many species are endangered by alteration of their habitats. Clear-cutting of forests in the northwest nearly made the northern spotted owl extinct.

These owls feed mainly on small mammals: squirrels, voles, rats, mice, and some birds and small snakes

barn owl

barred owl

boreal owl

great gray owl

great horned owl

long-eared owl

northern hawk owl

northern saw-whet owl

short-eared owl

snowy owl

spotted owl

These owls eat mammals and songbirds, as well as insects

eastern screech owl

western screech owl

People's ignorance of our impact on owls has brought about most of these problems. To ensure the survival of these tremendously beneficial birds, we must learn more about them and their needs. Owls are difficult to study. Their solitary and nocturnal habits, as well as their excellent camouflage, make them hard to find. They are, however, being observed more successfully. The use of night vision lenses has added greatly to our knowledge of owls. There has also been an increase in funding for owl study. Scientists are learning a lot about owls' needs by placing radio tags on young nestlings so that they can be followed. In addition, Congress has passed laws making it illegal to shoot owls. Anyone found guilty of killing an owl in the United States faces a heavy penalty and a stiff fine. The United States Fish and Wildlife Service and the United States Forest Service are working together to find solutions to the problems of habitat destruction. DDT has been banned in the United States, because it causes eggshells of all birds to become so thin they break in the nest. Unfortunately, DDT remains in the soil and continues to be a threat long after its use has been discontinued.

Perhaps one of the most important ways to help owls is to educate the public about their value as pest-control agents. Insect-eating owls control large insects, centipedes, and spiders much more efficiently than insecticides, and, given a chance, the magnificent rodent hunters will keep the huge rodent populations in grain-growing regions under control.

The owls below eat mainly moths, butterflies, caterpillars, beetles, and other insects

burrowing owl

elf owl

ferruginous pygmy-owl

flammulated owl

mountain pygmy-owl (red phase)

whiskered screech owl

vermiculated owl

37

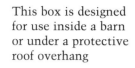

This box is designed for use inside a barn or under a protective roof overhang

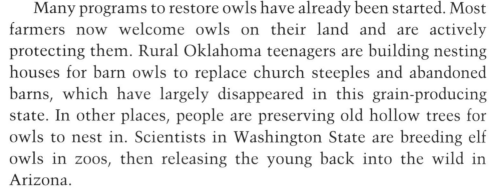

Many programs to restore owls have already been started. Most farmers now welcome owls on their land and are actively protecting them. Rural Oklahoma teenagers are building nesting houses for barn owls to replace church steeples and abandoned barns, which have largely disappeared in this grain-producing state. In other places, people are preserving old hollow trees for owls to nest in. Scientists in Washington State are breeding elf owls in zoos, then releasing the young back into the wild in Arizona.

Most owls are fairly competent at looking after themselves and don't do too badly in areas where they are left alone. Now that we realize humans have created most of the problems that threaten owls, let us hope we have the wisdom to continue to correct these problems, making it possible for these majestic pest controllers to prosper everywhere.

A Glossary of Owls

The range maps in the glossary that follows are approximate, giving the general outlines of the range of each species. Because they are mainly active at night, owls have not been studied as much as other birds, and it is possible that some species exist where they have not been spotted and recorded. Too, owls, like other birds, live where the environment is right for them. Their ranges can change as the ecological conditions around them change.

Different colors on maps indicate different subspecies. Lighter and darker shades show breeding, resident, and wintering areas when the information is available. Maps that are not labeled indicate that winter and summer ranges are the same. Some owls, such as the barn and great horned, are resident in their ranges all year. Other owls move south when winter becomes severe.

Barn Owl

(*Tyto alba*—Greek *tuto*, a night owl, and Latin *alba*, white.) This 14- to 21-inch-long, 13- to 17.5-ounce brown-and-white owl has a heart-shaped face. It hunts in open fields or parks. Its favorite food is small rodents, but it will eat any small mammal up to the size of a young jackrabbit. Barn owls' most often heard call is a loud screaming *shreeee* uttered in flight. They nest in old buildings, attics, church steeples or belfries, and sometimes caves or holes in riverbanks. Their five to eleven eggs are incubated for thirty-two to thirty-four days. Chicks fly eight to ten weeks after hatching.

wingspan 43 in

Tyto alba pratincola

Tyto alba lucayana

Tyto alba furcata

Tyto alba guatemalae

Barred Owl

(*Strix varia*—Latin *strix*, owl, and Latin *varia*, varigated, referring to its plumage.) This heavily barred brown owl is the noisiest owl of North America. Its calls are extremely varied. It is sometimes called the hoot owl because its territorial call is a low-toned *HOO-hoo-to-HOO-oooo, HOO-hoo-hoo-to-WHOO-ooooo*, which is often translated as "Who cooks for you, who cooks for you all?" Though this 16- to 24-inch-long, 14- to 23-ounce owl is often heard, it is seldom seen. It lives in wooded swamps and dense forests. It hunts small rodents up to the size of squirrels, and snakes, lizards, and small birds. Its two to four eggs are laid in abandoned crow or hawk nests or natural tree cavities and incubated twenty-eight to thirty-two days. Young fly forty to forty-five days after hatching.

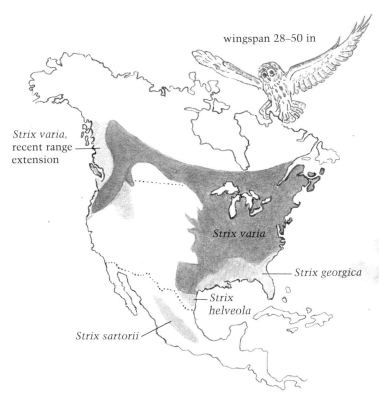

wingspan 28–50 in

Strix varia, recent range extension

Strix varia

Strix georgica

Strix helveola

Strix sartorii

Boreal Owl

(*Aegolius funereus*—Greek *aigolos*, a nocturnal bird of prey, and Latin *funereus*, funeral, referring to the tolling bell-like quality of its voice. *Boreal* means "of the north.") This small (8- to 12-inch-long, 7- to 8-ounce) owl lives in dense northern woods. It hunts for small mammals—voles, lemmings, and mice —in the nearby grasslands from a perch at the edge of the forest. The courtship song of this deep brown owl is a soft, pleasant, bell-like *TINGG-TINGG-TINGG-TINGG-TINGG-TINGG-TINGG*. Its four to seven eggs are laid in an abandoned woodpecker hole and are incubated twenty-five to twenty-seven days. Young fly about thirty-two days after hatching.

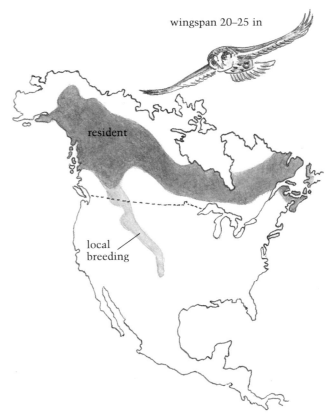

wingspan 20–25 in

resident

local
breeding

Burrowing Owl

(*Speotyto cunicularia*—Greek *speos*, cave or grotto, and Latin *cunicularius*, a burrower.) The burrowing owl was formerly placed in the genus *Athene*, but recent genetic testing showed it belongs in a genus of its own. This small (8.5- to 11-inch-long, 6.5- to 7.8-ounce) brown owl is unusual. It has very long, lightly feathered legs and a short, stubby tail; it runs about on the ground like a roadrunner; and, unlike most owls, it tends to be active during the daytime. It hunts moths, amphibians, snakes, lizards, insects, and scorpions on the treeless prairies of western North America, Florida, and the West Indies. Its most often heard call is a dovelike *coo-coo-ROOOO! coo-coo-ROOOO!* Its seven to nine eggs are laid in old mammal burrows, or in burrows it has dug itself, and are incubated three to four weeks. Young fly in forty-five days. The burrowing owl is threatened by rodent poisoning, insecticides, and habitat destruction.

wingspan 20–24 in

breeding area

resident

Speotyto cunicularia hypugaea

Speotyto cunicularia floridana

Speotyto cunicularia hispaniola

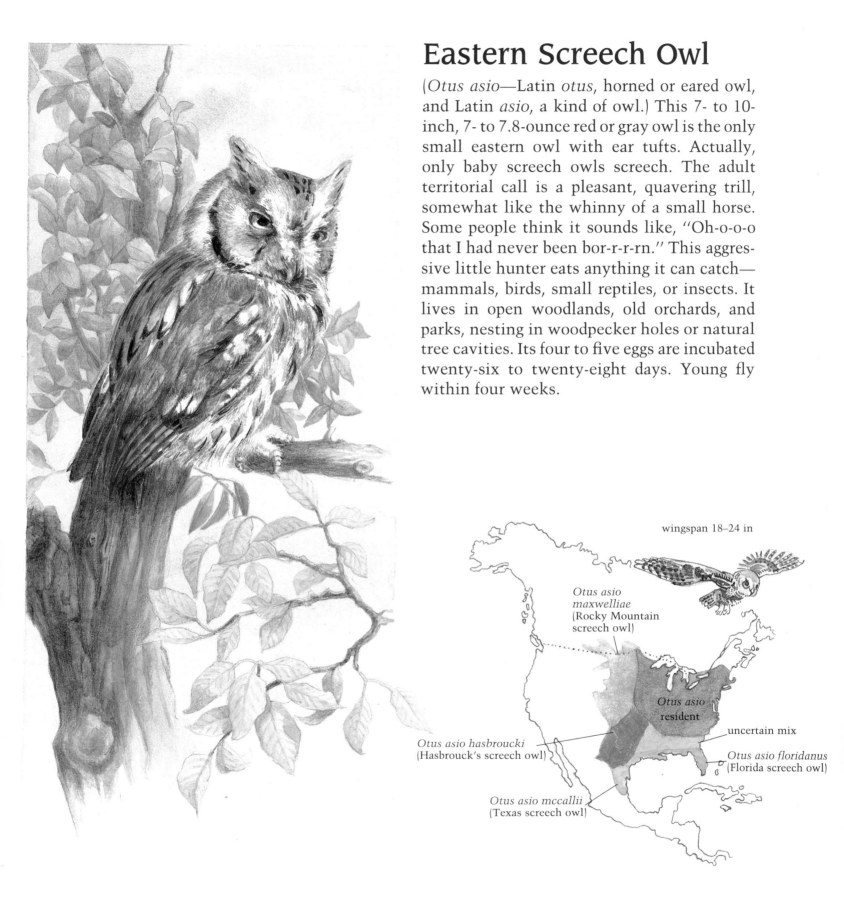

Eastern Screech Owl

(*Otus asio*—Latin *otus*, horned or eared owl, and Latin *asio*, a kind of owl.) This 7- to 10-inch, 7- to 7.8-ounce red or gray owl is the only small eastern owl with ear tufts. Actually, only baby screech owls screech. The adult territorial call is a pleasant, quavering trill, somewhat like the whinny of a small horse. Some people think it sounds like, "Oh-o-o-o that I had never been bor-r-r-rn." This aggressive little hunter eats anything it can catch—mammals, birds, small reptiles, or insects. It lives in open woodlands, old orchards, and parks, nesting in woodpecker holes or natural tree cavities. Its four to five eggs are incubated twenty-six to twenty-eight days. Young fly within four weeks.

wingspan 18–24 in

Otus asio maxwelliae (Rocky Mountain screech owl)

Otus asio resident

uncertain mix

Otus asio hasbroucki (Hasbrouck's screech owl)

Otus asio floridanus (Florida screech owl)

Otus asio mccallii (Texas screech owl)

Elf Owl

(*Microthene whitneyi*—Named in honor of J. D. Whitney, American geologist, and Greek *micros*, small, and Athena, goddess of wisdom.) This tiny (5- to 6-inch-long, 1- to 1.4-ounce) gray owl is the smallest North American owl. It eats large insects, spiders, scorpions, and small reptiles, catching its prey on the wing, on the ground, or in bushes in scrub-wooded canyons and giant saguaro cactus forests of the arid southwest. Its most common call is a rapid, high-pitched *whi-whi-whi-whi-whi-whi, chewk-chewk-chewk.* It most often lays two to four eggs in old gila woodpecker holes in saguaros and incubates them twenty-four days. Young leave the nest at twenty-eight to thirty-two days. These owls are doing well where cactuses are left undisturbed.

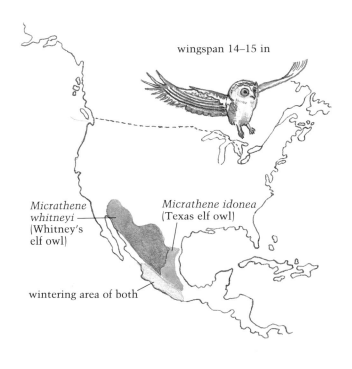

wingspan 14–15 in

Micrathene whitneyi (Whitney's elf owl)

Micrathene idonea (Texas elf owl)

wintering area of both

Ferruginous Pygmy-Owl

(*Glaucidium brasilianum*—Probably from Greek *glaukidion*, glaring, in reference to its eyes, and Latin *brasilianum*, of Brazil, where the first specimen was found.) The common name of this little (6.5- to 7-inch-long, 2.8- to 3.1-ounce) owl means "rusty." While all ferruginous pygmy-owls are a rusty brown, some are more reddish and others are more grayish. This owl's most commonly heard call is a series of short, sharp, pulsating whistles, *khuit-khuit-khuit, pruik, pruik, pruik.* This spunky and fearless little hunter eats insects, a few desert birds, and small rodents. It lives in mesquite thickets, in saguaro cactus desert, and along riverbanks, laying its three to five eggs in woodpecker holes in trees or cactuses. Eggs are incubated twenty-eight days. Owlets fly within thirty days after hatching. These owls are rare in the United States but plentiful in Mexico.

wingspan 15–16 in

Glaucidium cactorum
(cactus pygmy-owl)

Glaucidium ridgwayi
(southern ferruginous pygmy-owl)

Flammulated Owl

(*Otus flammeolus*—Latin *otus*, a horned or eared owl, and Latin *flammeolus*, a small flame, referring to its color.) This tiny (6- to 7-inch-long, 4.4- to 5.2-ounce) owl is the smallest eared owl in North America. Some flammulated owls are gray and some are reddish. The owl gets its name from the V-shaped reddish bars running down the wings in gray birds and from the varigated red-brown color of reddish birds. Its call, a low-pitched, mellow *who-WHOOP!*, is often heard along the edges of western mountain woodlands and forest. This owl eats mostly insects caught on the wing and spiders, caterpillars, and scorpions. It migrates in winter to areas where insects can be found. It lays its two to four eggs in abandoned woodpecker holes, incubating them twenty-five days. Owlets fly within twenty-five days after hatching.

wingspan 14–19 in

breeding area

wintering area

Great Gray Owl

(*Strix nebulosa*—Latin *strix*, a kind of owl, and Latin *nebulosa*, clouded, in reference to the color of its plumage.) This large (24- to 33-inch, 45- to 53.3-ounce) ash-gray owl is the longest of the North American owls. It has a huge round head with enormous facial disks, a long tail, and long, broad wings. Its fluffy plumage makes it look even bigger. Its most common call is a very deep *WHOOOO-OOO-OOO-OOO WHOOOO-OOO-OOO-OOO WHOOOO-OOO-OOO-OOO*, repeated eight to ten times. It lives in tundra areas and dense forests of the north and eats any small animal it can catch, but prefers rodents. It nests in abandoned hawk or crow nests or broken stumps of tall trees, and incubates its two to four eggs twenty-eight to thirty days. Owlets fly in eight weeks.

wingspan 54–60 in

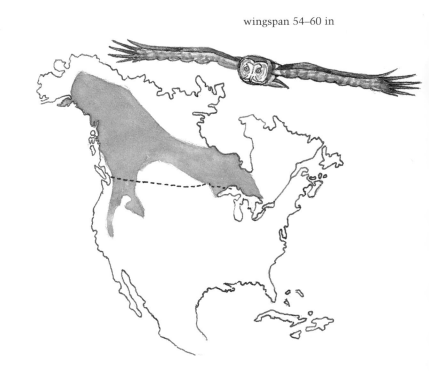

Great Horned Owl

(*Bubo virginianus*—Latin *bubo*, a horned or hooting owl, and Latin *virginianus*, from Virginia.) This 18- to 25-inch, 50.7- to 65.7-ounce owl is the second largest North American owl. It is the only large North American owl with ear tufts. It is the best known of the large owls because it lives throughout all of North America. It is often called a hootie or hoot owl because its most often heard call is a deep, resonant *HOO! who-who-who HOO-HOO!* that can be heard several miles away. It will eat anything, even skunks, but prefers rodents or rabbits. It lays two to three eggs in old hawk, crow, heron, or eagle nests and incubates them for twenty-five to thirty days. Young fly in nine to ten weeks.

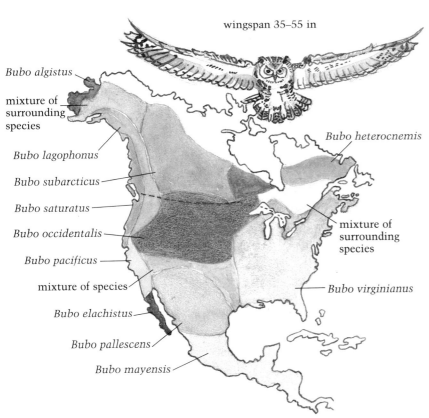

wingspan 35–55 in

Bubo algistus

mixture of surrounding species

Bubo lagophonus

Bubo subarcticus

Bubo saturatus

Bubo occidentalis

Bubo pacificus

mixture of species

Bubo elachistus

Bubo pallescens

Bubo mayensis

Bubo heterocnemis

mixture of surrounding species

Bubo virginianus

Long-eared Owl

(*Asio otus*—Latin *asio*, a kind of owl, and Greek *otus*, eared.) This 13- to 16-inch, 9- to 11.7-ounce mottled brown and tawny owl has large burnt-orange facial disks and long, closely spaced ear tufts. It lives in wooded areas near open country where it hunts for rodents. It probably has more calls than any other owl. Its most common call is a soft, musical *kwooo-kwooo-kwooo-kwooo*. Its three to five eggs are laid in abandoned nests of other birds of prey and incubated twenty-one to twenty-eight days. Young fly in thirty-five days. Long-eared owls migrate south in winter.

wingspan 36–42 in

northern breeding area

breeding area

southern wintering area

Mountain Pygmy-Owl

(*Glaucidium gnoma*—Greek *glaucidium*, glaring, and Greek *gnomon*, to have knowledge, in reference to its supposed intelligence.) This owl was formerly grouped with *Glaucidium californicus* as the northern pygmy-owl. However, recent genetic tests show that they are separate species. This 5.5- to 6.5-inch, 1.5-ounce owl is slightly smaller than the northern pygmy and has a shorter tail. Like the northern pygmy-owl, it has two large black spots resembling eyes on the back of its head. It hunts insects and small vertebrates along forest edges. Its voice is a low, muted, dovelike cooing, *OOOO-oooo, OOOO-oooo.* It lays its three to six eggs in abandoned woodpecker holes and incubates them twenty-two days. Young fly within thirty days.

wingspan 14.2–14.5 in

51

Northern Hawk Owl

(*Surnia ulula*—Greek *surnion*, a kind of owl, and Latin *ulula*, crying out as if in pain.) This medium-sized (14- to 17-inch, 8- to 9.6-ounce) dark chocolate brown and creamy white owl looks and acts like a hawk but has facial disks. One of its calls is a rolling whistle, *ulululululululul*. Its most common call is *tu-WHITTA-WITT tu-WHITTA-tu-WITT tuh-WHITTA-WHITTA*. It lives in northern evergreen forests and bogs and hunts by day, preying on small rodents, mostly voles. It nests in hollow stumps of dead trees, old woodpecker holes, or abandoned hawk or crow nests. It incubates its five to six eggs twenty-five to twenty-eight days. Young fly by thirty-five days.

wingspan 31–35 in

southern wintering area

Northern Pygmy-Owl

(*Glaucidium californicum*—Greek *glaucidium*, glaring, and Latin *californicum*, of California, where the first specimen was found.) Also called California pygmy-owl. Formerly classed as a subspecies of *G. gnoma* until recent genetic tests showed they were separate species. This 7- to 7.5-inch, 1.5- to 1.8-ounce owl is larger than the mountain pygmy-owl. It may be either grayish brown or rusty brown with white underparts. It has two large, black, oval-shaped spots resembling eyes on the back of its head. This aggressive little hunter holds its long tail at a perky angle. It hunts mountain highland forest clearings for insects, birds, and small vertebrates. Its call is a clear, whistled *too-too, too-too, too-too*. It lays two to six eggs in abandoned flicker or woodpecker holes and incubates them twenty-eight days. Young fly within thirty days.

wingspan 14.2–16 in

53

Northern Saw-whet Owl

(*Aegolius acadicus*—Greek *aegolos*, a nocturnal bird of prey, and Latin *acadicus*, of Acadia, a former French colony of southeastern Canada where the bird was first seen.) Some say this little (7- to 8.5-inch, 3.6- to 4.3-ounce) reddish-brown-and-white owl was named for its courtship call, which is supposed to sound somewhat like whetting a saw: *SWEEE-awwww SWEEE-awwww*. Others suggest its name comes from the French word *chouette* (shoo-ET), meaning "small owl." Its most common call is a series of rapid whistled notes—*too, too, too, too, too*—up to 130 a minute. This cuddly little owl lives in forests bordering wetlands where it hunts for woodland rodents. Northern individuals migrate south in winter. It lays five to six eggs in tree cavities, mostly old woodpecker holes, and incubates them twenty-five to thirty days. Young fly by five weeks.

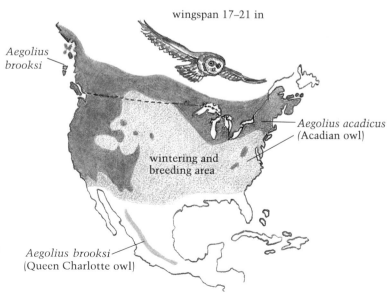

wingspan 17–21 in

Aegolius brooksi

Aegolius acadicus (Acadian owl)

wintering and breeding area

Aegolius brooksi (Queen Charlotte owl)

Short-eared Owl

(*Asio flammeus*—Latin *asio*, a kind of owl, and Latin *flammeus*, flame-colored, referring to its rusty plumage.) The ear tufts of this crow-sized (13- to 17-inch, 10- to 15-ounce) buff-and-brown owl are barely visible. One of nature's best predators, this owl hunts for mice and other rodents by slowly patrolling open grasslands. It is relatively quiet and hunts mainly in the daytime. Its territorial call is a low-pitched *voo-hoo-hoo-hoo-hoo*. Its four to seven eggs are laid in shallow scrapes on the ground and are incubated twenty-four to twenty-eight days. Owlets fly within thirty-five days. These owls migrate far south to avoid bad weather and poor food supplies.

wingspan 38–44 in

Snowy Owl

(*Nyctea scandiaca*—Greek *nycteus*, nocturnal, and Latin *scandiaca*, of Scandinavia, where it was first identified.) This 3.5- to 4.4-pound, gray-spotted white owl is the heaviest of the North American owls. The exceptionally dense insulating plumage covering its 21- to 30-inch-long body keeps it warm in the cold tundra of northern Canada. It hunts either day or night, mostly for lemmings (mouselike animals), but it can kill animals as large as foxes. When its food supply gets low, it migrates into the central United States. Its territorial call is a series of great booming notes, *WHOOO-WHOOOO-WHOOOO AAOW*, which carry long distances. It lays five to fourteen eggs (depending upon the availability of lemmings) in a shallow scrape on the ground and incubates them thirty-two to thirty-four days. Young fly in sixty days.

wingspan 54–56 in

breeding area

normal southern
wintering area

wintering vagrants

Spotted Owl

(*Strix occidentalis*—Latin *strix*, a kind of owl, and Latin *occidentalis*, western.) This brown-eyed, 16- to 19-inch, 13.7- to 20.7-ounce brown-and-white-spotted owl is closely related to the barred owl. It is endangered because of destruction of its habitat, the coniferous forests of the west coast. It eats flying squirrels, wood rats, insects, and birds. Its common call, *hoo-hoo-oou-hooAAWWW*, sounds something like a baying hound. Its two to four eggs are laid in crevices, caves, or tree cavities. They are incubated twenty-five to twenty-eight days. Young fly in six weeks.

wingspan 42–45 in

Strix occidentalis caurina

Strix occidentalis

Strix occidentalis lucida

Vermiculated Screech Owl

(*Otus vermiculatus*—Latin *otus*, a horned or eared owl, and Latin *vermiculatus*, worm-like, referring to its markings.) Very little is known about this 8- to 9-inch-long, tawny and reddish-brown owl whose lower parts are indistinctly vermiculated (marked with wavy outlines resembling worm tracks). It is strictly nocturnal and lives mainly in dense wooded areas of tropical and subtropical habitats from northwestern Mexico to Bolivia. This owl has small ear tufts, which usually lie flat; yellow eyes; and long, bare toes. Its call is a long trill on one pitch like a spadefoot toad's call, starting softly and gradually swelling, then cutting off abruptly. It suffers from destruction of its habitat in Mexico.

wingspan unknown

Western Screech Owl

(*Otus kennicottii*—this species was named for Robert Kennicott, first director of the Chicago Academy of Sciences, and Latin *otus*, a horned or eared owl.) This gray to gray-brown owl is quite similar to the eastern screech owl but has more prominent dark markings on its back and breast, and red phases are rare. There are eight subspecies and the size varies with location. Those in the north may be 11 inches long; those in the southern range are smaller. These owls will eat almost any small mammal, bird, or insect they can catch. They inhabit a great variety of open woodlands and scrub from southern Alaska to central Mexico, sometimes even nesting in urban areas. Their territorial song is a series of hollow, bouncing-ball whistles rising in pitch and ending in a brief roll. This owl's two to five eggs are laid in natural tree cavities or abandoned woodpecker holes in trees or saguaro cactuses. They are incubated twenty-six to twenty-eight days. Young fly at four weeks.

wingspan 18–24 in

Otus kennicottii kennicottii (Kennicott's screech owl)

Otus kennicottii bendirei (California screech owl)

Otus kennicottii yumanensis (Yuma screech owl)

Otus kennicottii cardonensis

Otus kennicottii vinaceus

Otus kennicottii xantusa

Otus kennicottii suttoni

Otus kennicottii aikeni (Aiken's screech owl)

uncertain

Whiskered Screech Owl

(*Otus trichopsis*—Latin *otus*, a horned or eared owl, and Greek *trix*, hair, plus Greek *opsis*, having the appearance of, referring to the long whiskerlike bristles on its face.) This 6.5- to 8-inch, 5.6- to 6.5-ounce red-brown or gray owl is similar to the western screech owl but is smaller and more coarsely mottled. It eats mostly large insects and caterpillars. It is usually found in dense mountain forests. Its most common call is a series of short, mellow hoots, *whoot-whoot-whoot-WHOOT-whoot*. Its three to four eggs are laid in natural tree cavities or abandoned flicker nests and are probably incubated about the same length of time as those of the western screech owl. Young fly in about a month.

Pandora
moth larva

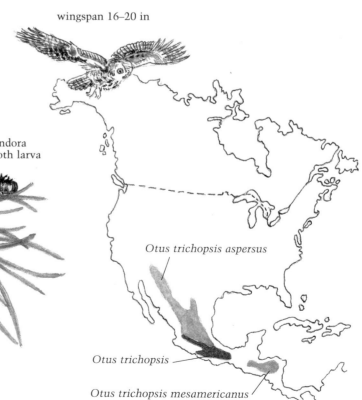

wingspan 16–20 in

Otus trichopsis aspersus

Otus trichopsis

Otus trichopsis mesamericanus

North American Owls
Listed by Family, Genus, and Species

CLASS AVES; ORDER STRIGIFORMES

Strigidae

One of the two families of owls. Strigidae have stocky bodies, short necks, large round heads, round facial disks, large eyes, hawklike bills, and rounded tails. They range from 5 to 33 inches in length and from 1 ounce to 4.4 pounds in weight. Most eat rodents or other small mammals, birds, or insects. Most are nocturnal or twilight hunters. There are twenty-one species representing ten genera (*Aegolius, Asio, Bubo, Glaucidium, Micrathene, Nyctea, Otus, Speotyto, Strix,* and *Surnia*) living in North America.

GENUS *Aegolius*
Boreal Owl   *Aegolius funereus*
Northern Saw-whet Owl   *Aegolius acadicus*

GENUS *Asio*
Long-eared Owl   *Asio otus*
Short-eared Owl   *Asio flammeus*

GENUS *Bubo*
Great Horned Owl   *Bubo virginianus*

GENUS *Glaucidium*
Ferruginous Pygmy-owl   *Glaucidium brasilianum*
Mountain Pygmy-owl   *Glaucidium gnoma*
Northern Pygmy-owl   *Glaucidium californicum*

GENUS *Micrathene*
Elf Owl   *Micrathene whitneyi*

Genus *Nyctea*
Snowy Owl   *Nyctea scandiaca*

GENUS *Otus*
Eastern Screech Owl   *Otus asio*
Flammulated Owl   *Otus flammeolus*
Vermiculated Screech Owl   *Otus vermiculatus*
Western Screech Owl   *Otus kennicottii*
Whiskered Screech Owl   *Otus trichopsis*

GENUS *Speotyto*
Burrowing Owl   *Speotyto cunicularia*

GENUS *Strix*
Barred Owl   *Strix varia*
Great Gray Owl   *Strix nebulosa*
Spotted Owl   *Strix occidentalis*

GENUS *Surnia*
Northern Hawk Owl   *Surnia ulula*

Tytonidae

One of the two families of owls. Tytonidae are large-headed birds with heart-shaped facial disks, dark eyes, and long, feathered legs. These strictly nocturnal owls eat mostly mice and rats. They live throughout the temperate range. Only one species, *Tyto alba*, lives in North America.

GENUS *Tyto*
Barn Owl   *Tyto alba*

Bibliography

AMADON, DEAN, AND JOHN BULL. *Hawks and Owls of the World: A Distribution and Taxonomic List*. Los Angeles: Western Foundation of Vertebrate Zoology, 1988.

BERGMAN, CHARLES. "Face-to-Face with the Stalwart Imp of Cactus Country!" *Smithsonian* (December 1984): 122–30.

BRADY, IRENE. *Owlet the Great Horned Owl*. N.p.: Bradybooks, 1984.

BULL, EVELYN L., AND MARK G. HENJUM. "The Neighborly Great Gray Owl." *Natural History* (September 1987): 32–41.

CASSIDY, JAMES, AND OTHERS. *Book of North American Birds*. Pleasantville, New York: Reader's Digest, 1990.

DE LA TORRE, JULIO. *Owls: Their Life and Behavior*. New York: Crown Publishers, 1990.

ECKERT, ALLAN W. *The Owls of North America (North of Mexico)*. New York: Doubleday and Company, 1974.

GEHLBACK, FREDERICK R. "Odd Couples of Suburbia." *Natural History* (June 1986): 56–66.

HAYWARD, PATRICIA, AND GREGORY D. HAYWARD. "Lone Ranger of the Rockies." *Natural History* (November 1989): 79–84.

HEINRICH, BERND, ADAPTED BY ALICE CALAPRICE. *An Owl in the House: A Naturalist's Diary*. Boston: Little Brown and Company, 1990.

JOHNSGARD, PAUL A. *North American Owls: Biology and Natural History*. Washington, D.C.: Smithsonian Institution Press, 1988.

NERO, ROBERT, ALETA KARSTAD, AND FREDERICK W. SCHUELER. *Wilderness Album Series: Owls in North America*. Winnipeg, Canada: Hyperion Press, 1987.

QUINTON, MICHAEL S. "Life of a Forest Hunter: The Great Gray Owl." *National Geographic* (July 1984): 122–36.

ROWE, MATTHEW. "The Owl That Traded a Hoot for a Hiss." *Natural History* (May 1989): 32–42.

SPARKS, JOHN, AND TONY SOPER. *Owls: Their Natural and Unnatural History*. New York: Facts on File, 1989.

UDVARDY, MIKLOS D. F. *The Audubon Society Field Guide to North American Birds*. New York: Alfred A. Knopf, 1977.

VOOUS, KAREL H. *Owls of the Northern Hemisphere*. Cambridge, Massachusetts, 1988.

WALTON, RICHARD K., AND ROBERT LAWSON. *Birding by Ear: Eastern*. Peterson Field Guides 38. Boston: Houghton Mifflin Company, 1990.

_____. *Birding by Ear: Western*. Peterson Field Guides 41. Boston: Houghton Mifflin Company, 1990.

WILSON, BARRY W. *Reading From Scientific American: Birds*. San Francisco: W. H. Freeman and Company, 1979.

WOLFE, ART. "Long-eared Owls: Masters of the Night!" *National Geographic* (January 1980): 30–34.

ZIM, HERBERT S. *Owls*. New York: William Morrow and Company, 1977.

Index

Page numbers in *italics* indicate illustrations.